THE PERFORMANCE MANAGEMENT POCKETBOOK

By Pam Jones

Drawings by Phil Hailstone

"The difficulty about being a market leader is staying there. This pocketbook offers help and advice in doing just that."
Nick Fox, Country Manager, Kodak Ltd

"This pocketbook closes the gap between what managers do and what their people can achieve."
Graham Baker, Human Resources Controller, Ladbroke Racing Ltd

Published by:
Management Pocketbooks Ltd
14 East Street, Alresford, Hants SO24 9EE, U.K.
Tel: +44 (0)1962 735573   Fax: +44 (0)1962 733637
E-mail: pocketbks@aol.com
http://members.aol.com/pocketbks

This edition published 1999

ISBN 1 870471 65 2

British Library Cataloguing-in-Publication Data – A catalogue record for this book
is available from the British Library.

Printed in U.K. by: Alresford Press Ltd, Prospect Road, Alresford, Hants

WHO SHOULD READ THIS BOOK

This book is for managers who care about their people and want to succeed through them and with them. It provides a clear understanding of performance management and practical tips and techniques to think about issues such as:

- Communicating the organisational goals
- Setting clear objectives
- Understanding the impact of your own style
- Creating a climate for good performance
- Coaching and delegating effectively
- Dealing with performance issues
- Motivating and empowering others
- Creating high-performance teams

CONTENTS

WHAT IS
PERFORMANCE MANAGEMENT?

WHAT IS PERFORMANCE MANAGEMENT?

COMMON MISCONCEPTIONS

What is your definition of performance management?

Most people associate it with concepts such as:

- Appraisal
- Performance-related pay
- Targets and objectives
- Motivation and discipline

Yet, performance management is much
more than this.

WHAT IS PERFORMANCE MANAGEMENT?

A DEFINITION

Performance management is about getting results. It is concerned with getting the best from people and helping them to achieve their potential.

It is an approach to achieving a shared vision of the purpose and aims of the organisation. It is concerned with helping individuals and teams achieve their potential and recognise their role in contributing to the goals of the organisation.

SHIFTS IN PERFORMANCE MANAGEMENT

The approach to performance management has changed over recent years and it is now recognised that enhancing individual and team performance will contribute to bottom-line results.

Shifts in performance management	
From	**To**
An annual event	A continuous process
Assessment only	Assessment and development
Superficial evaluation of personality	Specific evaluation of behaviour
Loosely associated with the business cycle	Closely related to the business plan
Superficial objectives	Specific objectives

THE PERFORMANCE MANAGEMENT TOOLKIT

In order to manage both their own performance and that of their team, managers need a toolkit of techniques and skills - 'tools' that work together to help individuals, teams and the organisation excel.

But, like a master craftsman, you need to know how and when to use each of the management tools.

All the tools in this toolbox are covered in this Pocketbook.

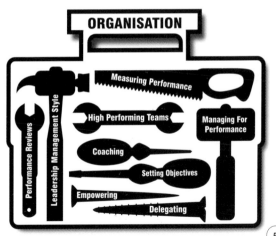

ORGANISATION

Measuring Performance

High Performing Teams

Managing For Performance

Coaching

Setting Objectives

Empowering

Delegating

Performance Reviews

Leadership Management Style

5

THREE GOOD REASONS TO GET STARTED

If you only want three good reasons for developing your knowledge and approach to performance management, remember that it will help to:

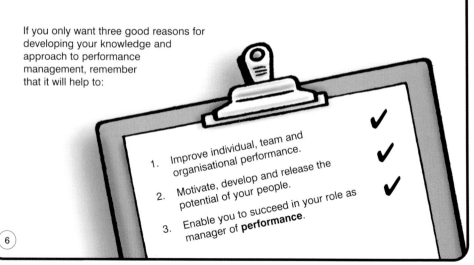

1. Improve individual, team and organisational performance.

2. Motivate, develop and release the potential of your people.

3. Enable you to succeed in your role as manager of **performance**.

WHAT IS PERFORMANCE MANAGEMENT?

GETTING TO THE HEART OF
THE ORGANISATION

Performance management gets to the very heart of the organisation. It needs to reflect and support the organisation's culture, strategy and style.

It is the way to communicate to people:

- What is expected of them
- What they will be rewarded for
- How they should deliver results
- What results the organisation is looking for on a business-wide scale

A CONSISTENT APPROACH

Effective performance management requires a consistent approach to:

- Leadership
- The way individuals are treated
- The way teams operate
- The performance management systems used
- The culture, purpose and strategy of the organisation

Is this the approach your organisation takes?

AN INCONSISTENT APPROACH

Inconsistency can lead to problems such as:

- No clear direction, weak values and weak performance culture
- Vague and inequitable objectives
- Variable and unfair appraisal/review, leading to a lack of improved performance and motivation
- Inadequate provision for training and development
- Poor communications due to bureaucracy

Or is this the approach your organisation takes?

CASE EXAMPLE 1

Problem Consider a sales organisation which recognises that customer service is vital in maintaining competitive advantage. An extensive customer service training programme is completed, yet customer feedback indicates that there has been little improvement.

Reasons This is because targets and incentives were based on volume of sales and not service. People will always focus their efforts on the areas of work for which they are rewarded.

Solution The reward system needs to be altered to reflect the emphasis on service. It also needs to recognise the contribution of all members of the team, including back-office support.

CASE EXAMPLE 2

Consider the organisation which advocates empowerment, passing responsibility down the line, yet fails to achieve this new approach.

The leadership style at the top of the organisation remains autocratic. Mistakes and risk-taking are not tolerated. Employees are not given the skills necessary to adjust successfully to the new approach.

For it to work, empowerment requires trust from the top, training and coaching, and a different focus for incentives and rewards.

CREATING A SENSE OF MISSION

For performance management to work well, organisations need to have a clear picture of where they are going. This means communicating their purpose, strategy, the values they adhere to, and the standards of behaviour they expect from their employees. If an organisation is clear about these issues, it can communicate them to the employees through its performance management systems*.

Campbell & Gould: 'Mission Vision and Strategy Development'.
Financial Times Handbook of Management, FT/Pitman, London 1985

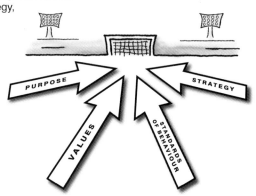

ALIGNING FOR SUCCESS

A well-planned and implemented approach to performance management can achieve
this sense of mission by providing:

- Clarity on the organisation's overall goals
- A framework for linking strategies and priorities to jobs
- Greater clarity on role requirements and support to employees
- Recognition of success and regular feedback
- A clear basis for promotion
- A framework for development and improvement

AN ORCHESTRA IN TUNE

An organisation with a consistent approach to performance management is like a first-class orchestra.

A first-class orchestra is well conducted and clear about the symphony it is playing.

The instruments are all in tune and the musicians know their roles and the tempo to follow.

They reach a crescendo together and enjoy the process.

LEADING
FOR PERFORMANCE

THE IMPORTANCE OF LEADERSHIP

Leadership is critical to the achievement of high performance, no matter what your business or area of responsibility. It is also essential in helping others aspire to and attain high levels of performance for themselves and the organisation.

WHAT MANAGERS SAY

Leadership is:

> *'Having a clear focus, communicating it to others and giving them the space to develop.'*

> *'Bringing people with you - engendering commitment and enthusiasm.'*

> *'Setting strategic objectives and being creative in helping others achieve against those objectives.'*

> *'Being accountable and responsible and ensuring financial profitability and success.'*

What is your definition of leadership?

A POPULAR MODEL

One of the most popular approaches to leadership is the idea of transactional and transformational leadership, developed by James McGregor Burns.

Transactional Leadership	Transformational Leadership
Clarify goals and objectives to obtain immediate results	Establish long-term vision
Create structures and processes for control	Create a climate of trust
Solve problems	Empower people to control themselves; manage problem-solving
Maintain and improve the current situation	Change the current situation
Plan, organise and control	Coach and develop people
Guard and defend the culture	Challenge and change the culture
Power comes from the position and authority in the organisation	Power comes from influencing a network of relationships

ANALYSING YOUR COMPETENCIES

Leading for performance requires that you recognise both the transactional and the transformational aspects of leadership, to bring out the best in your people.

This questionnaire will help you to assess your leadership competencies. You can also give it to other people, to understand more about their perception of your leadership approach.

Please indicate the extent to which each of the statements on the following page applies to you. Think about each statement and rate yourself according to the 5-point scale below, where:

    5 = always
    4 = often
    3 = sometimes
    2 = rarely
    1 = never

ANALYSING YOUR COMPETENCIES
QUESTIONNAIRE

#		
1.	Listen carefully to others	1 2 3 4 5
2.	Give people responsibility for tasks and projects	1 2 3 4 5
3.	Challenge the rules and conventions in the organisation	1 2 3 4 5
4.	Have a clear vision for the team	1 2 3 4 5
5.	Have a clear perception of your strengths and weaknesses	1 2 3 4 5
6.	Encourage ideas from the team	1 2 3 4 5
7.	Demonstrate trust to others	1 2 3 4 5
8.	Anticipate and adapt to changing conditions	1 2 3 4 5
9.	Communicate the vision and ideas clearly to others	1 2 3 4 5
10.	Spend time keeping up to date and developing new skills	1 2 3 4 5
11.	Motivate and encourage others	1 2 3 4 5
12.	Provide training to enable people to work effectively	1 2 3 4 5
13.	Help others to manage change	1 2 3 4 5
14.	Demonstrate a high level of commitment in your work	1 2 3 4 5
15.	Manage time well	1 2 3 4 5
16.	Develop a good communication network throughout the organisation	1 2 3 4 5
17.	Provide support for people when needed	1 2 3 4 5
18.	Manage stress well	1 2 3 4 5
19.	Focus on achieving results	1 2 3 4 5
20.	Have a positive attitude towards yourself	1 2 3 4 5

ANALYSING YOUR COMPETENCIES

SCORING THE QUESTIONNAIRE

Q	Column 1 score	Q	Column 2 score	Q	Column 3 score	Q	Column 4 score	Q	Column 5 score
1		2		3		4		5	
6		7		8		9		10	
11		12		13		14		18	
16		17		18		19		20	
Total		Total		Total		Total		Total	

The leadership competencies contained in this questionnaire cover skills and behaviours associated with modern leadership, and can be classified under these headings:

Column 1 **L** istening
Column 2 **E** mpowering
Column 3 **A** dapting
Column 4 **D** elivering
Column 5 **S** elf-understanding

LEADING FOR PERFORMANCE

L.E.A.D.S.

Leading for performance means that you have to:

L isten   to others to understand their thoughts, concerns and aspirations

E mpower   others by giving them responsibility backed up by trust, training and support

A dapt   to changing situations and always be ready to listen to and implement new ideas

D eliver   high-quality results by setting clear goals and objectives which are linked to end results

S elf-understand   as the more you can understand yourself and your impact on others, the easier it is for you to manage yourself and adapt your style to bring out the best in others

WORK CLIMATE

The work climate is simply a way of describing how the workplace feels to those in it. It is influenced by the inter-relationships between people, the way the responsibilities are distributed, the way communication is managed, how decisions are made and the physical setting in which work takes place.

LEADING FOR PERFORMANCE

IS YOUR TEAM CLIMATE SUNNY OR STORMY?

Sunny	**Stormy**
People are allowed to take initiative	People feel boxed in
Team work flourishes	There is friction and lack of appreciation between team members
People understand their contribution	People have little understanding of their role
There is a clear direction and good communication	There are conflicting goals and mixed messages
Workload is distributed evenly, taking account of individuals' skills and abilities	Work is spread unevenly amongst the team
Skills, abilities and motivation of team members are recognised	There is little understanding of what makes team members tick
Physical work environment is conducive to good performance	Physical environment prevents good performance

LEADING FOR PERFORMANCE

TIPS FOR IMPROVING THE WEATHER

If you want to improve the climate in your team:

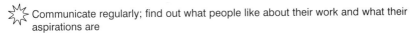 Communicate regularly; find out what people like about their work and what their aspirations are

☀ Create a shared vision so that everyone knows where they are going

☀ Improve the physical environment; changes can have a real effect on morale

☀ Use ideas from the team to make improvements to the way you all work

☀ Use people to their strengths; consider people's skills, abilities and aspirations, and allocate work accordingly

(25)

MANAGING YOUR OWN PERFORMANCE

To manage the performance of others, you need to:

- Be aware of your impact on others
- Be clear about your priorities
- Manage your time in a whole-life sense
- Manage your stress levels

'Your first and foremost job as a leader is to take charge of your own energy and then help orchestrate the energy of those around you.'
Peter F. Drucker

LEADING FOR PERFORMANCE

UNDERSTANDING YOUR IMPACT ON OTHERS

To understand your impact on others:

- Gain feedback from friends and colleagues
- Use a 360° feedback questionnaire
- Analyse your strengths and weaknesses and compare them to other successful leaders in your organisation
- Find a mentor who can help you understand yourself
- Ask yourself what impression you and your office would give to a complete stranger

Through this process of feedback and reflection, think about:

- The impression you would like to make
- How you could adjust or adapt your approach to get the best out of yourself and others

SETTING PRIORITIES

This exercise will help you to think further about how you manage your own performance.

Instructions:

Using a sheet of blank paper, draw an image at the centre to represent your job. Draw some main branches off this, to represent elements of your job, and then some smaller branches to elaborate on each of your key roles.

(Pete's mind map on page 30 provides an example)

You now have a **mind map** of your job.

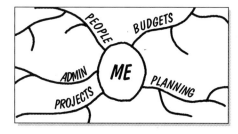

SETTING PRIORITIES

MIND MAP ANALYSIS

Analysing the mind map will help you to understand how you are managing your current performance and what you need to focus on in the future. Use the following questions to help you in the analysis:

- Looking at the key roles, what percentage of your time do you spend on each? (Note onto your mind map.)

- Indicate on your mind map which tasks you like (+ + +) and dislike (– – –). The degree of liking or disliking can be indicated by the number of pluses or minuses.

- Now consider your personal effectiveness, ie: which tasks are you good at?

- Circle the tasks which you could delegate to others.

- Identify areas where you would benefit from some training and development.

SETTING PRIORITIES

PETE'S MIND MAP

Pete is an IT manager. He works for the IT director in a medium-sized organisation which processes insurance claims. He always feels overworked and as if he is reacting to problems rather than preventing them.
This is Pete's mind map.

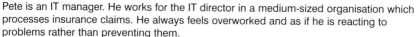

SETTING PRIORITIES

PETE'S APPROACH

When Pete analysed his mind map, he realised that he needed to delegate more and coach his people to take on more responsibility. This would leave Pete with more time to focus on the overall scheduling for his department and take a more pro-active role.

He also realised that he needed to manage upwards and influence the IT strategy and resources available to his team.

Finally, he decided that he needed some training and development in the area of IT strategy and influencing skills.

SETTING PRIORITIES

TAKING ACTION

What messages is your map giving you about how you manage your own performance and what you could do to enhance it? Note down your actions for:

1. How will you spend your time?
2. What will you delegate to others?
3. How will you manage your career?
4. What training and development activities will you plan for yourself?

MANAGING YOUR TIME & YOUR LIFE

To manage your time in a meaningful sense, identify the things you value in life (eg: career, health, family, friends, learning, travel, etc) and build them into your daily **To Do** list.

When people are clear about what is really important to them, they can incorporate it into their overall approach to time management.

As Sir John Harvey Jones says:

DAILY TO-DOs

SHORT-TERM GOALS

LONG-TERM GOALS

VALUES

"I will always need to believe that my work is worthwhile and of value, but now I know that there are many other things in my life which matter more. This feeling freed me to tackle risks and to stick to my belief in ways which I now realise actually made me more likely to move ahead rather than the reverse."
*'Making it Happen, Reflections on Leadership', **Sir John Harvey Jones, 1994.***

MANAGING YOUR STRESS LEVELS

We all feel stressed at times. The secret lies in balancing your energy levels with the challenges you are facing.

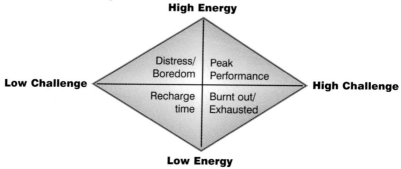

UNDERSTANDING STRESS LEVELS

Peak performance   Your energy levels match the challenge at hand. Be aware that peak performance is not always sustainable over long periods of time.

Burnt out   Your energy levels do not match the challenge at hand - you are exhausted.

Distress   You are not being challenged. This can also cause stress.

Recharge   Recharge time is important at the end of each day to ensure that you have time for peace and relaxation.

Where are you right now? Can you plan your life so that it has a good balance between energy and challenge, and can you build in some recharge time to help?

NOTES

PERFORMANCE MANAGEMENT SKILLS

PERFORMANCE MANAGEMENT SKILLS

DELEGATING

WHY MANAGERS DON'T DELEGATE

Delegation is often seen as a difficult area.

- How do you delegate effectively?
- What sorts of things can you delegate?
- How can you ensure that they will be completed to your own high standards?
- Is it quicker to do it yourself?
- Are your people capable?
- Is your team already too busy?
- What will you do if you delegate everything?

These are just a few of the issues explaining why managers don't delegate.

PERFORMANCE MANAGEMENT SKILLS

DELEGATING

FIVE-STEP PROCESS

The five-step process for **planned delegation** provides a way of getting work done and also a way of motivating and developing people to bring in fresh ideas.
This, in turn, will develop greater trust and a
climate for success within the team.

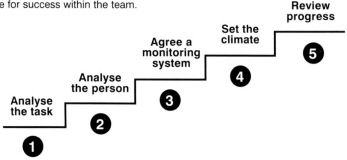

Review progress **5**

Set the climate **4**

Agree a monitoring system **3**

Analyse the person **2**

Analyse the task **1**

PERFORMANCE MANAGEMENT SKILLS

DELEGATING

STEP 1: ANALYSE THE TASK

- Identify tasks you are unlikely to complete on your own and mark a portion or all of them for delegation.
- Are there any longer-term projects which you could delegate whilst they are still in the development stage?
- Will the task provide the individual with some sort of challenge or are you just delegating things which don't really require delegating?
- Who else will you need to inform if you are delegating a task which involves others?
- How can you ensure that the individual will have the right degree of authority and responsibility to achieve the task?
- Can you link delegation to coaching and development?

This diagram may help you to understand which tasks are suitable for delegation, by looking at which quadrant they fit into.

DELEGATING

STEP 2: ANALYSE THE PERSON

- Who are the team members most suitable for delegation?
- What workload do they have? Do they have the resources, knowledge and skills to achieve the task?
- Will it dovetail into work they are already doing?
- What's in it for them? Will it help their development, provide them with greater visibility or provide a coaching opportunity?

Try to stretch people but don't break them. The challenges provided by delegation can be motivational but, if handled badly, can be stressful and threatening.

PERFORMANCE MANAGEMENT SKILLS

DELEGATING

STEP 3: AGREE A MONITORING SYSTEM

- Involve the individual in the setting up of the monitoring system
- Agree goals and targets for what you want to achieve by when
- You may need to break the task down into stages or sub-tasks
- Both parties need to be clear about what is being delegated and what is not
- Define clear success criteria so that you both know what quality standards are required and what the end result should look like
- Agree times to review progress; this will vary according to the task and the confidence of the individual

DELEGATING

STEP 4: SET THE CLIMATE FOR DELEGATION

- Listen to ideas from the person to whom you are delegating; he or she will often bring a fresh perspective to the situation

- Keep the communication channels open at all times so the person can approach you if problems are encountered

- Build in praise and feedback along the way so that the individual feels appreciated, and ensure that credit is given for the work done

- Don't interfere between review periods; you need to build trust and show that you can empower the individual

- Build in coaching and development opportunities where necessary so the person has the skills and abilities to complete the task

PERFORMANCE MANAGEMENT SKILLS

DELEGATING
STEP 5: REVIEW PROGRESS

- Review progress on a regular basis
- Provide support and guidance
- Ask searching questions to help the individual think things through rather than provide all the answers
- When the task is completed review the progress against the success criteria you set earlier
- Review the learning, identifying any new skills and competencies that have been acquired and any new learning goals for the future
- Gain feedback on your role; consider if there is anything else you could do in the future to improve your delegation

COACHING

Coaching involves helping individuals or teams to develop and reach their full potential. Coaching can usually take place at work. There may be a task that you, as manager, need to delegate or something you currently do which could be a learning opportunity for someone else. It may be something looming in the future, a project or a presentation which would provide a developmental challenge to one of your team.

It is also important to focus on the people you wish to coach:

- What do they need to do to develop further?
- Do they have a performance gap?
- Is there something they do well which you could build on?

THE COACHING PROCESS

Matching the needs of the manager with those of the individual being coached requires careful planning. This can be agreed and developed during the initial coaching meeting.

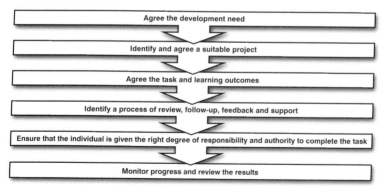

Agree the development need

Identify and agree a suitable project

Agree the task and learning outcomes

Identify a process of review, follow-up, feedback and support

Ensure that the individual is given the right degree of responsibility and authority to complete the task

Monitor progress and review the results

COACHING SKILLS

Coaching requires managers to use a whole range of skills. They need to be aware of:

- Their own approach and influence on the people they are coaching
- The style and needs of those being coached; this means thinking about:
  - their development needs
  - the way they learn best
  - possible pitfalls and problems

In addition, managers need to hone three key skills in order to coach effectively. These are:

1. Listening   2. Questioning   3. Feedback

COACHING SKILLS: LISTENING

Look at the learner; use good eye contact and open body language to show you are listening

Interruptions - avoid them so you can give 100% of your attention

Summarise regularly so that you are both clear about what you have agreed and how you will progress with the coaching project

Time - allow sufficient; coaching requires regular meetings to monitor and review progress

Encourage the person to talk and come up with options and ideas to move the project forward

Nurture an environment of trust where the individual can feel free to contribute and ask questions which they know will be dealt with in an objective and supportive manner

COACHING SKILLS: LISTENING

In coaching, you need to listen not only to the thoughts and ideas being spoken but also to the feelings and emotions being expressed and the intentions and commitment the learner has to the issue at hand.

Listening to thoughts requires:

- Listening to **all** the words that are being spoken; we often listen selectively and get side-tracked on issues which are of more importance to us
- Identifying the data that the learner has collected and used
- Understanding the learner's approach and logic in working the issue through
- Summarising and using the learner's words to reflect back his or her ideas and thoughts

COACHING SKILLS: LISTENING

Listening to feelings requires:
- Listening to the way in which the learner presents his or her ideas
- Asking yourself:
  - Is their tone confident or concerned?
  - Is their body language positive and open, or defensive and closed?
  - Is their eye contact clear and direct, or shifting and avoiding?
  - Is the pace fast, or slow and faltering?

Listening to intentions requires:
- Listening to what the learner intends to do about the situation
- Establishing what the learner's conclusions and judgements are about the situation
- Identifying what the learner wants
- Measuring the level of the learner's commitment

Good listening, therefore, requires that you listen with all your senses. Using the skills effectively can pay real dividends.

COACHING SKILLS: QUESTIONING

Asking questions is an important area of coaching. Questions can be used to:

- Help the learner develop ideas
- Explore all the options available
- Encourage the learner to think through all the issues
- Help the learner take ownership for the coaching project
- Motivate the learner further, as the individual realises that he or she has the ability to complete the task

COACHING SKILLS: QUESTIONING

We often focus on what is wrong and what isn't working with questions such as:

- What is your problem?
- How long have you had it?
- Who's to blame?
- Why haven't you solved it?
- What will you do about it?

It's much more positive to focus on outcomes and what can be achieved with questions such as:

- What do you want?
- How will you know when you have achieved it?
- What else will you improve?
- What resources do you already have?
- Is there something similar in which you have already succeeded?
- What's the next step?

Adapted from ITS Teaching Seminars 1996

COACHING SKILLS: G.R.O.W. MODEL

The **G.R.O.W.** model is a questioning approach to coaching which builds on positive questioning.

The model guides the coach to ask the learners questions about:

Goals   Are they clear about what they want to achieve?
Have they set any sub-goals along the way?
Are the goals realistic and measurable?

Reality   Where are they right now with the project?
What is helping or hindering the process?
Is there anyone they can learn from?

Options   What are the options available?
Are there any other possibilities?
Which is the most appropriate option?

Will   What is their level of commitment?
If commitment is low, would they be better off focusing their energy elsewhere?
What would be the consequences of this?

Adapted from 'Coaching for Performance', John Whitmore, Nicholas Brealey, 1996.

(53)

PERFORMANCE MANAGEMENT SKILLS

COACHING SKILLS: GIVING FEEDBACK

Feedback is essential throughout the coaching process for both the coach and the learner. The coaches will benefit from feedback on their role and the learners will require feedback to know how they are progressing, what they are doing well and where they could improve. A useful way of thinking about feedback is to use **BOOST**:

Balance   Include positive elements as well as reflecting on areas for improvement.

Observed   What you have seen them do; focus on behaviour not personality.

Ownership   Both parties must own the feedback for it to be useful and actionable.

Specific   Try to keep the feedback specific and factual so that it is clear and understandable.

Time   Pick the appropriate time to give feedback and give it in an atmosphere of trust.

It is often best to start by asking those concerned how they think they are doing - they will usually be very honest about their performance and you will only have to add to or confirm their ideas.

COACHING SKILLS: RECEIVING FEEDBACK

For anyone receiving feedback, it can be a difficult process. Remember:

- Don't get defensive
- Ask questions to clarify the feedback and explore the issue further
- Don't ignore praise; take it on board
- It's your choice to accept or reject the feedback offered
- Work out what you can do with the feedback, how it can help you to improve your performance
- Remember to say thank you (feedback is not always easy to deliver)

DEALING WITH POOR PERFORMANCE

We all have people who are not performing to standard, but try not to label them as 'poor' performers. Over their careers, people may have times when they are performing well and other times when they are not bringing in the results you expect. Your challenge is to maintain and develop the performance of all your people.

One of the main issues is when to act. Managing poor performance is a bit like catching sand falling through an hourglass. You need to tackle the grains rather than wait for a heap of sand to build up.

WHEN TO TACKLE POOR PERFORMANCE

Look at the diagram opposite.
When would you need to act?
Consider four factors:

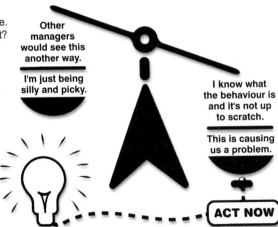

Other managers would see this another way.

I'm just being silly and picky.

I know what the behaviour is and it's not up to scratch.

This is causing us a problem.

ACT NOW

POOR PERFORMANCE CONSIDERATIONS

1. **I know what the behaviour is and it's not up to scratch.** Can you define exactly what behaviour is causing you concern? Could you describe it to a third party? A feeling is not enough; specific examples are needed rather than generalisations.

2. **This is causing us a problem.** Is the behaviour just irritating or is it having a definite impact on the business? Is money being wasted or other staff being upset? You must demonstrate that it is detrimental.

3. **Other managers would see this another way.** Am I interpreting this the right way? Would another manager accept this as reasonable and am I being eccentric?

4. **I'm just being silly and picky.** My personal dislike of untidy desks is not really fair. It doesn't always mean that the person must be disorganised. I'm putting too much emphasis on too little evidence and personal idiosyncrasies.

Only when you have satisfied yourself in all four areas is it time for action. You must be sure that you are dealing with a real problem which others would see objectively in the same light.

REASONS FOR THE PERFORMANCE GAP

There may be a number of reasons for the poor performance.

1. **Personal ability:** Has the individual the capability? Is there a skills gap needing training?

2. **Manager ability:** Have I given enough direction, and made sufficient resources available?

3. **Process gap:** Has the appraisal system been at fault? Have the goalposts moved or external forces made the task unattainable? Have there been regular enough review sessions and is the reward system pointing in the right direction?

4. **Environmental forces:** Has the organisation created departmental barriers, red-tape overkill, cultural restrictions or hidden agendas which make the task impossible?

5. **Personal circumstances:** Has something at home affected performance at work?

6. **Motivation:** Is the person demotivated or suffering from stress or lack of challenge?

Poor performance can often be a symptom of other problems. Obviously, you need to work with the individual concerned to recognise where the problem is and how it should be resolved.

DEALING WITH POOR PERFORMANCE

- Discuss the issue, providing clear feedback and explaining the consequences of continued poor performance
- Try to get to the root of the issue; establish the real cause of the poor performance
- Explore all the options and alternatives available to help bring the person back on track
- Agree the next steps and set clear objectives for improvements; establish regular review meetings to monitor progress
- Provide training and coaching if appropriate
- Monitor and document progress; several short-term hiccups may point to a more deep-seated problem requiring firmer action

Help them up or help them out - don't ignore the problems.

MOTIVATING

There is a whole range of motivational theories but the secret to motivation is to understand your people.

- People are motivated by different things at different stages of their lives
- You have a greater influence than you may realise in motivating your people

In America, 46% of those who quit their jobs last year did so because they felt unappreciated. *(US Department of Labor)*

PERFORMANCE MANAGEMENT SKILLS

HOW TO MOTIVATE OTHERS

- Allow the individuals to develop their job, continually improving on their work
- Set targets so that the employee can gain a sense of achievement
- Give as much authority as possible to allow the employee free rein (empowerment)
- Give regular feedback to prevent misdirection of effort and bad feeling over external factors, making targets impossible
- Give praise and show appreciation
- Encourage teamwork to enhance a sense of belonging and develop valuable synergy from the contributions of the individuals within the group
- Ensure that the work environment is conducive to good performance

PERFORMANCE MANAGEMENT SKILLS

HOW TO MOTIVATE OTHERS

- Find out what drives each of the team members: people are different; make an effort to understand individual aspirations

- Don't assume that money is the only motivator; focus on extrinsic rewards can distract people from working to their full potential

- Realise that your own motivation will significantly influence that of others

- People will support what they help to create; give people variety and interest, and some control over what they do

  Operators in a manufacturing company were given control over their machines. They covered all the maintenance tasks with a resulting 50% improvement in machine downtime and eradication of oil leaks.

- Show trust and be open with people; keep them in the picture, not in the dark

EMPOWERING

> *"People you lead have to recognise that they too have power.*
> *The aim is for people to say: 'The leader did nothing, we did it ourselves'."*
> **Steve Shirley, Life President of FI Group**

Empowering literally means 'giving power'. It is the process of enabling others. By giving up power, you can actually gain more power and lead the organisation more effectively. However, the whole idea of giving up power can be a little frightening.

Empowerment need not entail surrendering your legitimate managerial authority, but it does represent a leap of faith. Empowerment is built around four elements:

1. Responsibility   **2. Trust**   **3. Training**   **4. Support**

THE FOUR ELEMENTS OF EMPOWERMENT

1. RESPONSIBILITY

People need to feel a sense of ownership and see the big picture of how their contribution fits into the organisational vision. This will help to develop their sense of responsibility (and value) to the organisation.

Tips:

Identify the areas where people could take on greater responsibility, eg:

- Evaluating others' work
- Planning and scheduling work
- Recruitment and training
- Presentations
- Holiday scheduling
- Determining the pace of work
- Setting targets

THE FOUR ELEMENTS OF EMPOWERMENT

2. TRUST

Trust is difficult to define. We know when it is there and we know when it is lacking. It is something that needs to be earned. To gain trust you need to be seen as working with integrity and honesty for the good of the team. The key ingredients for trust are:

- Credibility, consistency and dependability
- Honesty at all times
- Willingness to admit mistakes
- Openness and willingness to listen to the concerns and worries of others
- Willingness to share information and keep the bigger picture visible
- Giving accurate feedback on performance

How do you rate on this list? How would other people rate you and what can you do to build up your trust level.

THE FOUR ELEMENTS OF EMPOWERMENT

3. TRAINING

People cannot take on new responsibility without the tools to do the job. These may be technical skills concerning software or machine maintenance, or managerial skills like influencing or coaching. These competencies may be called **enablers** and the match of Enablement and Empowerment gives interesting results:

Entrenched Bunkers are people who lack power and autonomy. With no motivation, like shell-shocked soldiers, they retreat to the comfort of usual tasks when work becomes stressful.

Loose Cannons have power but not ability and leave their mark via misunderstandings and blunders, causing upset and cynicism toward empowerment.

Caged Eagles have the ability to perform but no authority. They are tied by organisational practices and are a vastly under-utilised resource.

Fully Empowered employees have the skills and authority to perform to their abilities. The individual is highly motivated and the organisation gains immensely from the extra contribution.

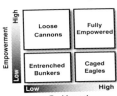

Barner, R, 'Enablement: The Key to Empowerment,' Training & Development, June 1994

THE FOUR ELEMENTS OF EMPOWERMENT

4. SUPPORT

Empowerment can be enhanced through providing support, spending time coaching, testing out ideas and allowing for mistakes. Most managers work under the umbrella of low-support/high-challenge, with a greater workload and no support from above. This often leads to burnout and low morale. What is needed is a high-support/high challenge scenario. To do this, you need to ask searching questions, challenging the individual, but provide support at the same time.

Supporting and challenging means:

- Saying 'thanks'
- Listening and questioning
- Challenging thinking and stretching ideas
- Giving feedback - positive and developmental
- Being open about your support to others
- Providing stretching objectives
- Providing coaching and development

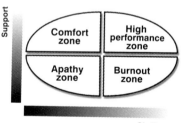

PERFORMANCE MANAGEMENT PROCESS

PERFORMANCE MANAGEMENT PROCESS

PERFORMANCE REVIEWS

Performance reviews are often seen as an extra burden. Yet, if managed well, they can be a positive and useful process providing you, the manager, and your people with the opportunity to discuss issues such as:

- Achievements over the past year
- Their current performance
- Objectives which will be set for next year
- Personal learning and development needs

- Longer-term career prospects
- Skills and experience which they are perhaps under-using

The real success of any appraisal lies in the interaction between the appraiser and appraisee and establishing a relationship that can be built upon throughout the year.
The performance review process can be divided into three stages:

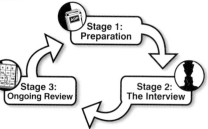

Stage 1: Preparation

Stage 2: The Interview

Stage 3: Ongoing Review

PERFORMANCE MANAGEMENT PROCESS

PERFORMANCE REVIEWS

STAGE 1: PREPARATION

Don't overlook the amount of time and effort you will need to give to the preparation to ensure a worthwhile appraisal.

- Make sure you have set aside enough time

- Make sure that you will be free from interruptions

- Ensure that the room layout is conducive to a relaxed one-to-one meeting

- Give plenty of notice to the appraisees so that they have time to prepare themselves for the meeting

- Spend time collecting the relevant data; this may involve talking to internal or external customers to obtain a valid view of their overall performance

- Finally, both parties need to prepare the relevant paperwork and review last year's objectives; this is an important process as it allows time to think through all the appropriate performance issues and provides a checklist of points to cover

71

PERFORMANCE MANAGEMENT PROCESS

PERFORMANCE REVIEWS
STAGE 2: THE INTERVIEW

The interview is the most important part of the process. If handled well, it is a valuable motivational and planning tool for the year ahead.

- Ensure that you spend some time putting the appraisee at ease
- Ask questions to encourage self-analysis
- Ensure that the meeting is a two-way process; this involves listening and exploring the appraisee's views and ideas
- Give helpful feedback which involves praising the good things but not ignoring areas of poor performance
- Spend time looking at the appraisee's performance during the year and then look ahead to the new goals and objectives which need to be set
- Make sure that you have also looked at development needs for the coming period and helped the appraisee think about how to develop him/herself for the future
- Try to let the appraisee summarise the discussion and make sure that you record all the agreements and action steps
- At the end of the appraisal interview, there is usually a certain amount of paperwork which needs to be completed; ensure that you allow enough time to do this

PERFORMANCE REVIEWS

STAGE 3: ONGOING REVIEW

The appraisal interview is just one part of the whole performance review cycle. Appraising performance should be ongoing and include:

Regular feedback People need to know how they are progressing and time should be set aside to communicate this with them. This means that at the next appraisal meeting you really can avoid the 'law of no surprises'.

Ongoing coaching This is an excellent way of helping individuals to develop through their work. Coaching projects can be set up as part of an individual's development plan. Interim meetings will also ensure that objectives are being met and that the individual is aware of their performance and progress and also of any change in terms of their targets and objectives.

Development and training These activities need to go on throughout the year so that the individual is equipped with the skills to do his or her job and to develop into new roles.

Remember, the performance appraisal process can be rewarding and genuinely helpful to both parties, by formalising an evaluation of the previous year's work and planning ahead for the next.

73

OBJECTIVE SETTING FOR RESULTS

Objectives need to be set at all levels of the business. This ensures commitment at the higher levels of management and clear goals and objectives at lower levels. This is often achieved through cascading the corporate or strategic objectives into individual jobs.

CORPORATE or STRATEGIC PLANS

BUSINESS PLANS

DEPARTMENTAL GOALS

TEAM GOALS

INDIVIDUAL OBJECTIVES

OBJECTIVES FOR GOOD OBJECTIVES

Linked to business priorities
The cascade approach described on the previous page links jobs at all levels.
Objectives must be regularly reviewed and updated as circumstances change.

Linked to results, not activities
This means that we are concerned with output not activities - the ends and not
the means.

Measurable and specific
Objectives must state what exactly is to be measured, and within that, define acceptable
levels of performance.

Challenging but attainable
Ideally, your people should set their own objectives. Often these will be tougher than if
set by the manager. They should be stretching, challenging and developmental. Weed
out unattainable objectives as these can be demotivating.

OBJECTIVES FOR GOOD OBJECTIVES

Matching experience and capability Objectives should take account of the individual's ability, experience, knowledge and any development plan in place.

Updated Certain things may occur which affect the objective being measured but which are out of the control of the jobholder. As a result, objectives must be regularly updated, taking account of the business environment.

Number of objectives Don't set too many objectives. It is better to focus on a few quality areas rather than a long list which is impossible to achieve.

Compatible upwards/downwards/sideways Objectives should not clash with other people's activities, so they need to be compatible upwards, downwards and sideways.

A software manufacturer has two departments sitting next to each other. The first department is responsible for developing new software and has target dates for issuing the product. The second department is responsible for quality and has objectives relating to customer complaints on use of the software. It is easy to see that the two departments have conflicting objectives and there is a potential for bad feeling as one department frustrates the other's objectives.

HARD & SOFT OBJECTIVES

Hard objectives can be measured clearly in terms of outputs such as turnover, profit, percentage increases, etc. Soft objectives define the difference between 'acceptable' and 'excellent' performance. Soft objectives cover areas where **the way the job is done** is as important as the quantitative results.

A hotel receptionist may be measured only in terms of the number of guests booked into and checked out of the hotel each day, and the ability to answer the phone within three rings. These would be the hard objectives. How welcome the guests felt and the telephone manner used are obviously key to the hotel's success. These would make up the soft objectives, more difficult to measure, owing to their qualitative nature, but very important nonetheless.

Often soft objectives are measured through:

- Customer feedback
- Surveys
- Complaints
- Mystery shoppers

However, these are not always personalised.

DEFINING SOFT OBJECTIVES

It is important to break down soft objectives into desirable behaviours, ie: a positive attitude for a hotel receptionist tells you little until it is broken down into:

- Politeness
- Smiling and good eye contact with the customer at all times
- Appearance as described in the handbook
- Calm and practical approach
- Good knowledge of the hotel's services and systems

The real secret with soft objectives is that even if they can't be measured in the strictest sense, they can always be described. Once you have a clear picture, it is easier to train, develop and provide specific feedback to each individual involved.

SELF-DEVELOPMENT OBJECTIVES

People need to focus on their own development - expanding their repertoire of skills in preparation for future assignments and opportunities. Development objectives can range from:

- Coaching projects
- Assignments which will develop a specific skill or ability
- Courses offered by the organisation or other providers
- Activities outside work which will aid development
- Self-study activities

Ideally, people should have at least one self-development objective per year.

SELF-DEVELOPMENT OBJECTIVES

EXAMPLES

Jo needed to learn how to deal with a broad range of people and, in particular, break tasks and instructions down into understandable terms. She negotiated with her employer to spend one afternoon per month teaching economics to secondary school pupils. This helped her to acquire the patience and skills to be able to clearly explain issues and tasks in the workplace.

John attended evening class to understand more about information technology and systems. He worked in a warehouse as a packer but recognised that IT skills were essential for the future.

Sue took on a role as school governor as a way of contributing to the community, but also developed her wider management skills.

Pat took on the role of organising a major sales conference for her company. This increased her network and profile amongst colleagues and clients, and developed her confidence and her skills in managing projects.

PERFORMANCE MANAGEMENT PROCESS

MEASURING PERFORMANCE

Objectives help you measure performance but **beware**:

- Are you measuring the right thing? Remember: what gets measured gets managed, but what gets measured is often what is easy to measure.
- Are there too many measures on which to focus?
- Are you using measurement in a negative, punitive way?
- Do people understand how the measures fit into the bigger picture?
- Are measures imposed or do employees have an input into the process?
- Are individual measures appropriate or would team measures be more suitable?
- Do you review and change measures as business priorities change?

TEAM-BASED MEASURES

If you wish to enhance team performance, develop some team measure (the team is usually best placed to do this). Measures can be set around:

- The overall objectives and targets for the team
- Quality objectives
- Customer satisfaction targets
- Absenteeism
- Skill levels for the team

It is important that individual and team objectives don't work against each other but complement the bigger picture. And, remember to celebrate team success!

BALANCED BUSINESS SCORECARD

Many organisations are trying to find ways of looking at performance measurement from a whole-business point of view. What a job-holder does in the short-term needs to tie in with long-term organisational goals, and understanding the linkage is the key to successful performance management.

The Balanced Business Scorecard (BBS) framework does just this, translating the organisation's vision into understandable objectives at every level in the organisation. It provides an instant snapshot of performance in four key areas, as the diagram shows. The same areas apply across both organisations and departments within organisations.

FINANCIAL PERSPECTIVE
How do we look to our stakeholders?

CUSTOMER PERSPECTIVE
How does our organisation look to our customers?

Business Strategy

ORGANISATION LEARNING
Are we able to sustain innovations, change and improve?

PROCESS PERSPECTIVE
How effective are our key business processes?

PERFORMANCE MANAGEMENT PROCESS

BALANCED BUSINESS SCORECARD

TIPS

- Measures in each area will vary depending on the particular organisation and its mission; in turn, these will vary according to the level being examined:
  - the BBS for a business unit will have measures relating to the organisation's mission
  - the BBS for a team will relate to the team's goals
  - the BBS for an individual will focus on that person's objectives
- Balance is the keyword: each area is equally important and there should be no more than four or five measures in each of the quadrants (try not to measure everything and lose focus in a myriad of targets)
- Involve people from across the organisation to develop measures
- The chosen measures must reflect the culture of the organisation (Are you people driven or technology driven? Do you measure product innovations or job satisfaction?) The messages to the employees will depend on the measures used.

PERFORMANCE MANAGEMENT PROCESS

CREATING YOUR OWN SCORECARD

You can create your own scorecard with your team.
First, you need to be clear about your team vision
and goals; then develop quadrants and
measures to support them.

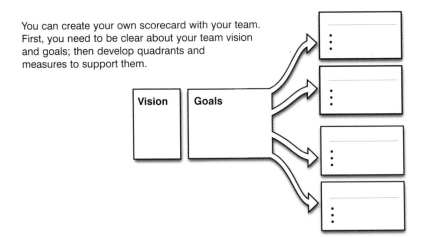

PERFORMANCE MANAGEMENT PROCESS

PETE'S SCORECARD

Remember Pete, the IT manager from page 30. He sat down with his team and worked through the process.

Vision
Provide the most effective and efficient IT solutions for the organisation

Goals
• Customer satisfaction
• Clear IT strategy
• Well-trained team
• Work within budget

Customer Satisfaction
• Reduce Stress
• Monitor Service
• Response Time
• Benchmarking

Business Focus
• IT Strategy
• Progress Review
• Business Application
• Managing Infrastructure

Team Learning
• Adequate Training
• Skills Audit
• Team Coaching
• Review Meetings

Financial
• Contractor Costs
• Software
• Capital Costs
• Outsourcing

He used the Balanced Business Scorecard to create objectives and measures for the team which fed directly into the team goals, vision and overall business objectives.

CREATING
HIGH-PERFORMING TEAMS

TEAMWORK IS IMPORTANT

We all work in teams. Some we see every day and others we communicate with via the internet, yet all are important to our success.

Think about the number of teams you are in:

- What is your role in each team?
- How effective are the different teams?
- What are the characteristics of the most effective teams?

We need to understand what makes good teamwork and replicate it elsewhere.

TEAMWORK IS IMPORTANT

Teamwork is vitally important. If teams are developed to perform well, they can:

- **Improve quality and productivity** - teams can set up and monitor processes and be mutually accountable for the results
- **Improve service** - a unified and consistent approach to service means that the whole team can focus on meeting customer needs
- **Decrease operating costs** - by improving productivity and workflow, bottom line benefits are realised
- **Encourage motivation and creativity** - teams often know best how to improve the way they work
- **Simplify job structures** - team members can support each other

CREATING HIGH-PERFORMING TEAMS

WHY TEAMS FAIL

If teams fail, it is often a result of one or more of the following:

Lack of support	If there is no support and encouragement from above, team morale will fade.
No clear purpose	Teams need clear goals and purpose so they know where they are going.
No team structure	Teams need structures and processes to manage their performance, ie: regular reviews, feedback systems and mechanisms for problem-solving.
Inappropriate systems	Performance management systems which encourage and reward individual performance can be detrimental to team performance.
Group think	Lack of diversity and a similarity in approaches and styles can prevent new ideas being introduced.
Hidden agendas	Are usually private and not declared and can prevent the team from moving ahead.
Conflicting views	Conflict can hold the team back but, if resolved, can lead to a collaborative approach.
Dominant v quiet members	All team members need to be involved for a team to work effectively.

CREATING HIGH-PERFORMING TEAMS

STAGES OF TEAM DEVELOPMENT

There are four stages of development which teams move through in order to achieve high performance:

1. **Forming** - when a team initially comes together.
2. **Storming** - often a difficult time when the team is working out roles and responsibilities.
3. **Norming** - involves setting rules and finding ways of working together. These give the team some identity and make the individuals more comfortable about the group.
4. **Performing** - once the rough edges have been knocked off the group and they have found a way of working together, they can really perform and take on the challenge of working together as a team.

Adapted from B.W Tuckman (1965) Development Sequence in small groups, Psychological Bulletin, 63, 284-499

WHAT DO HIGH-PERFORMING TEAMS DO?

When a team is performing really well, the members:

- Set high output and high quality targets
- Achieve targets and celebrate success
- Understand each other and appreciate differences
- Respect each other
- Are balanced in terms of the roles and skills they bring to the team
- Have responsibility and autonomy to achieve the results
- Are client orientated
- Regularly review and improve their performance
- Enjoy working together and are motivated to achieve

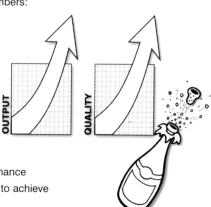

92

CREATING HIGH-PERFORMING TEAMS

TEAM EFFECTIVENESS QUESTIONNAIRE

Use the questionnaire that follows to find out if your team is performing at its best.
There are five areas to look at:

1. **Purpose** - Is it clear, understood and taken on with enthusiasm by members
   of the team?
2. **Performance** - Do the team members quantify their performance and are they
   happy with the results?
3. **Relationships** - Does everyone know, or at least appreciate, what each is bringing
   to the team and are the different roles recognised?
4. **Communication** - Are people listening to each other and do they feel confident
   enough to put forward their own views?
5. **Learning** - Does any individual or the whole team need more skills to work
   effectively?

You can give the questionnaire to members of your team to discover their views.

CREATING HIGH-PERFORMING TEAMS

TEAM EFFECTIVENESS QUESTIONNAIRE

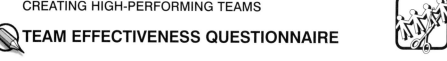

How would you rate your team on a scale of 1 - 5 (1 = not at all, 5 = very true)?

Purpose	We are committed to a common purpose	
	Our goals are clear, challenging and relevant	
	The purpose is aligned to the organisational strategy	
Performance	We know how we are doing	
	We get rewarded for achieving results	
	We know what the targets are and they're SMART	
Relationships	We get on really well	
	Each one of us is individually accountable	
	We bring different skills but each person's role is respected	

CREATING HIGH-PERFORMING TEAMS

TEAM EFFECTIVENESS QUESTIONNAIRE

Communication	We all express ourselves openly and honestly while the others listen	
	We do brainstorm and explore different ideas	
	We communicate well with the wider organisation	
Learning	Whenever we see a need, we arrange training	
	If necessary, we coach each other in certain areas	
	We review the team process and recognise our accomplishments	

What is the team really good at? What don't we do well? What can we do to improve?

CREATING HIGH-PERFORMING TEAMS

RUNNING A TEAM SESSION

If you have to run a team meeting, always try to ensure that the creativity and ideas of the team are included. You will need to think about how to use the meeting to get the most out of the team and the following tips may help.

- Let the team members have a chance to catch up with each other. Share progress and successes and use it as an opportunity to show your appreciation for their work.

- Introduce the discussion topic with background information (give the team prior notice of this so they have a chance to develop their ideas).

- Make sure everyone has a chance to voice his or her opinion. Use techniques such as brainstorming or buzz groups to generate ideas and bring in quieter members of the team. Keep an eye on the body language of the group, checking for signs of impatience, boredom, apathy and enthusiasm.

RUNNING A TEAM SESSION

- Summarise the thoughts of the group and check this is correct.

- Specify what decisions have been made and what actions will now occur. These may need documenting and circulating so people are clear what needs to be done and by when.

- Check if there is any unfinished business or other topics which need raising.

- Review the process of the group. What went well, not so well? How are the people feeling right now? What could be improved on for the next meeting?

In this way, you are managing not only the task issues in the meeting but also the process issues which lead to good teamwork.

DO'S & DON'TS OF FACILITATING

DO	DON'T
Prepare	Wing it
Keep a check on time	Let things run away
Use voice and body language to encourage ideas and show that you are listening	Use your position and power to push through your own agenda
Build on others' contributions	Shoot down ideas too readily
Get all relevant opinions	Take sides
Keep control of the discussion but allow all ideas to be heard	Be manipulative, condescending or dismissive
Generate enthusiasm	Appear tired of it all
Summarise and conclude	Leave things for next time
Review the process and agree on any improvements	Carry on with processes which are not producing the best results
Think about developing team members so that they can facilitate future meetings	Create an expectation that you will always drive the process

CREATING HIGH-PERFORMING TEAMS

WORKING WITH CROSS-CULTURAL TEAMS

Many teams now are global teams, made up of people of different nationalities and backgrounds. For these to work effectively:

- Allocate time to understanding and appreciating cultural differences
- Ensure that there is a common language that everyone understands
- Make sure there is good written documentation for people to work with and confirm their understanding
- When collecting ideas, allow people time to think them through and write them down
- Traditional brainstorming may not be appropriate, but Metaplan boards and Post-it notes for ideas could work well
- Remember to encourage input from everyone; in some cultures, junior members are not encouraged to speak out and it is not appropriate to criticise the boss
- As a team leader, do your homework first and understand the cultural issues and customs
- Create time for the team to socialise and understand each other

Remember, diversity, if handled well, can lead to greater creativity and synergy overall.

WORKING WITH VIRTUAL TEAMS

You are probably a member of one or more virtual teams. These are becoming more popular as IT allows people to work across departmental, geographical and national boundaries. To work effectively, virtual teams need:

- To exploit the best of IT communication systems; video-conferencing, e-mail, websites and voicemail all help
- Make sure the communication loop reaches everyone; no missed messages
- Check out any misunderstandings before reacting - if in doubt, speak to the person
- Create a culture of information sharing, but not overloading
- Develop an online team process review so that team members can express their ideas and concerns about how to work together
- Be aware of issues such as time differences, other commitments and priorities
- Keep dates set aside for conference calls, etc. when the team can share ideas verbally (be aware of time zones when you are setting up meetings)
- Try to meet at least once for some initial team-building, so that the team can develop a level of trust and mutual accountability; set up regular face-to-face meetings to keep the sense of team alive

BRINGING IT ALL TOGETHER

A SUMMARY

This Performance Management Pocketbook has provided a toolkit with a range of tools and techniques to help you to deliver high performance, through your team and in the organisation itself.

Yet, you need to make sure that you are using the tools in the right way, at the right time and with consistency.

HOW CONSISTENT IS YOUR APPROACH?

Do you:

- Develop an awareness of your impact on others?
- Always try to involve your people?
- Believe that teamwork is the best approach?
- Have a consistent management style?
- Spend time coaching and developing all team members?
- Work to build a positive climate in the team?
- Empower team members rather than control them?
- Develop appropriate performance review systems?
- Work with your people to set challenging, achievable and measurable objectives?
- Cascade and communicate the organisation's goals and strategy?
- Reward success and agree improvements?
- Provide regular feedback?
- Tackle poor performance?

REMEMBER

'Delivering high performance is a journey rather than a destination'

So, good luck and enjoy the trip!

FURTHER READING

- **Delivering Exceptional Performance**, Pam Jones, Joy Palmer, Carole Osterweil and Diana Whitehead, Times Pitman 1996

- **Coaching for Performance**, John Whitmore, Nicholas Brealey 1996

- **The Guidebook for Performance Management: Working with Individuals and Organisations**, Roger Kaufman, S. Thiagarajan, Paula Maggillis, Jossey-Bass Pfeiffer 1997

- **Managing for Performance**, Alasdair White, Piatkus 1996

About the Author

Pam Jones

Pam is Programme Director for the Performance Through People
Programme at Ashridge Management College. She has spent
three years working internationally with The Hong Kong and
Shanghai Banking Corporation and, more recently, has spent
time working in Australia with Monash Mt Eliza business school.
She has also written 'Delivering Exceptional Performance'
(FT Pitman 1996) and is a member of the editorial team for
Croners Publications. Her interest is in helping individuals,
teams and organisations excel.

Through her role at Ashridge and her own business, she works with a range of
organisations to contribute to their overall performance and development through
training, consultancy and one-to-one coaching.

Contact

Pam can be contacted at:
Ash Villa, 11 Tring Road, Edlesborough, Beds, LU6 2EQ U.K.   Email: pam.jones@ashridge.org.uk

Acknowledgements

This book is a reflection of some of my own learning and experience in the field of Performance
Management and I would like to acknowledge all the colleagues I have worked with over the years,
who have passed on their knowledge and who have worked creatively with me to develop new
ideas and approaches. Dave, my ever-patient husband, has played a valuable role in the editing of
material and made the whole project an enjoyable process.

THE MANAGEMENT POCKETBOOK SERIES

Pocketbooks

Appraisals Pocketbook
Assertiveness Pocketbook
Balance Sheet Pocketbook
Business Planning Pocketbook
Business Presenter's Pocketbook
Business Writing Pocketbook
Challengers Pocketbook
Coaching Pocketbook
Communicator's Pocketbook
Creative Manager's Pocketbook
Cultural Gaffes Pocketbook
Customer Service Pocketbook
Empowerment Pocketbook
Export Pocketbook
Facilitator's Pocketbook
Improving Profitability Pocketbook
Interviewer's Pocketbook
Key Account Manager's Pocketbook
Learner's Pocketbook

Managing Budgets Pocketbook
Managing Cashflow Pocketbook
Managing Change Pocketbook
Managing Your Appraisal Pocketbook
Manager's Pocketbook
Manager's Training Pocketbook
Marketing Pocketbook
Meetings Pocketbook
Mentoring Pocketbook
Motivation Pocketbook
Negotiator's Pocketbook
People Manager's Pocketbook
Performance Management Pocketbook
Project Management Pocketbook
Quality Pocketbook
Sales Excellence Pocketbook
Salesperson's Pocketbook
Self-managed Development Pocketbook
Stress Pocketbook
Teamworking Pocketbook

Telephone Skills Pocketbook
Telesales Pocketbook
Thinker's Pocketbook
Time Management Pocketbook
Trainer Standards Pocketbook
Trainer's Pocketbook

Pocketfiles/Other

Leadership: Sharing The Passion
The Great Presentation Scandal
Trainer's Blue Pocketfile of
Ready-to-use Exercises
Trainer's Green Pocketfile of
Ready-to-use Exercises
Trainer's Red Pocketfile of
Ready-to-use Exercises

Audio Cassettes

Tips for Presenters
Tips for Trainers

ORDER FORM

Your details	Please send me:	No. copies

Your details

Name _____

Position _____

Company _____

Address _____

_____

_____

Telephone _____

Facsimile _____

E-mail _____

VAT No. (EC companies) _____

Your Order Ref _____

Please send me:

The Performance Management Pocketbook ☐

The _____ Pocketbook ☐

The _____ Pocketbook ☐

The _____ Pocketbook ☐

The _____ Pocketbook ☐

Order by Post

MANAGEMENT POCKETBOOKS LTD
14 EAST STREET ALRESFORD HAMPSHIRE SO24 9EE UK

Order by Phone, Fax or Internet
Telephone: +44 (0)1962 735573
Facsimile: +44 (0)1962 733637
E-mail: pocketbks@aol.com
http://members.aol.com/pocketbks

Customers in USA should contact:
Stylus Publishing, LLC, 22883 Quicksilver Drive,
Sterling, VA 20166-2012 Telephone: 703 661 1500
Facsimile: 703 661 1501 E-mail: styluspub@aol.com